A New True Book

RIVERS

By Norman and Madelyn Carlisle

This "true book" was prepared
under the direction of
Illa Podendorf,
formerly with the Laboratory School,
University of Chicago

CHILDRENS PRESS, CHICAGO

Fox River, Illinois

PHOTO CREDITS

Reinhard Brucker—2, 20 (top), 28, 43 (top left)

James P. Rowan—4 (2 photos), 9, 15, 19, 20 (bottom), 22, 36, 39 (2 photos)

Bill Thomas—Cover, 7, 24, 25, 34

Jerry Hennen—10, 14, 18 (left), 31, 43 (bottom, 2 photos), 45 (2 photos)

M. Cole—16, 18 (right)

Julie O'Neil—26

Pat Michalski—32

Lynn Stone—43 (top right)

Melaine Ridtich—44

Len Meents—maps 8, 11, 12, 40, 41

COVER—Yellowstone River

Library of Congress Cataloging in Publication Data

Carlisle, Norman V., 1910-
   Rivers.

   (A New true book)
   Revised edition of: The true book of rivers. 1967.
   Summary: Describes how a river begins and grows and how it influences the land that it flows through. Also discusses the many ways people use rivers and the importance of keeping them clean and unpolluted.
   1. Rivers—Juvenile literature. [1. Rivers]
I. Carlisle, Madelyn. II. Title.
GB1203.8.C37   1982   551.48'3   81-38448
ISBN 0-516-01645-8   AACR2

TABLE OF CONTENTS

How Rivers Begin... 5

River Basins... 10

Rivers Change the Land... 14

Dams... 27

How We Use Rivers... 32

Rivers Are Water Highways... 38

We Need Clean Rivers... 42

Words You Should Know... 46

Index... 47

Rio Grande

Vermilion River, Illinois

HOW RIVERS BEGIN

Most rivers start high in mountains or hills. Some start in lakes or ponds. Others start with springs that bubble up from the ground.

The place where a river starts is its source.

A river starts as a little stream that flows downhill. Rain and melting snow run into it. More little streams join it. The river gets wider and wider.

The streams that join a river are called its tributaries.

Altamaha River, Georgia

Amazon R.

South
America

The mighty Amazon
River in South America
begins as a small stream
in the Andes Mountains. It
is the second longest river
in the world.

The Thames River in
England begins as a
meadow spring.

Source of the Mississippi River in Lake Itasca State Park

In the United States, the
Mississippi River starts in
a small lake in Minnesota.

RIVER BASINS

Rivers drain the land by taking the extra rainwater to the sea or ocean.

Almost half the United States is drained by streams and rivers that run into the Mississippi.

Mississippi River

The land drained by a
river and its tributaries is
called a river basin, or a
watershed.

At the edge of each watershed another one begins. A high ridge separates two watersheds. This ridge is called a divide.

CONTINENTAL
DIVIDE

The long high ridge of the Rocky Mountains, in the western United States, makes the Continental Divide. Some rain falling near the divide flows west toward the Pacific Ocean.

Rain falling just an inch or two away flows east toward the Atlantic Ocean.

Drinking from a mountain stream

RIVERS CHANGE THE LAND

Steams starting near a
high divide rush downhill.
Trees and other plants on
a watershed help hold and
store the water that falls
on it. Water rushing over

Big
Thompson
River
Canyon

bare ground carries soil
and rocks with it. Rocks
are bounced and tumbled
along until they are worn
smooth. Some are broken
up into stones and sand.

15

Yellowstone
River

When a river reaches level ground it moves slowly. It twists and turns to find the easiest way to go. That is why a slow-flowing river has many bends. As a river slows down it may drop some of its stones and sand and make an island.

A river flowing over soft soil carries away some of the soil. Rain and melting snow run down the slopes beside the river and wash more soil into it.

As a river wears away the land on both sides, it makes a valley. A river valley can be many miles wide.

Above: Waterton River, Montana
Right: Virgin River, Zion National Park, Utah

When a river cuts a path through hard rock, it makes a gorge. A gorge has steep rocky walls. The hard rock banks do not wash away as fast as soft soil does.

Genesee River Gorge, Letchworth State Park, New York

A mountain stream that
flows into the Rhine River
has cut a gorge almost
two thousand feet deep.
The sides of this gorge are
so close together in some
places that a man can
jump across the top.

Grand Canyon

A river flowing through softer rock cuts more of it away. Wind, rain, and blowing sand wear away more of the rock. That is what the Colorado River did. It made the Grand Canyon, the biggest canyon in the world. It is a mile deep and eight miles across in some places.

Middle Falls on the Genesee River

A waterfall is a river tumbling over a cliff. Most of the time, a river makes its own cliff. A river flows across hard rock for a while. Then it comes to a place where the rock is softer. The soft rock wears away faster. The riverbed becomes deeper here.

Great
Falls
of the
Potomac

Now the water drops
and hits the soft rock
harder than it did before.
More and more of the soft
rock wears away. After
thousands of years the
river may fall hundreds of
feet.

24

When a river flows into a quiet sea, it is suddenly slowed down. The river drops most of the soil it is carrying. This soil piles up. This new land is called a delta.

Mississippi River Delta

The city of New Orleans
is built on the delta made
by the Mississippi River.

One of the most famous
deltas in the world was
made by the Nile River in
Egypt. The Nile is the
longest river in the world.

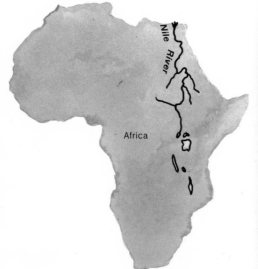

Victoria Nile, Uganda

DAMS

Heavy rains and melting snow can make a river rise until it floods the land. Houses are carried away. Bridges are torn down. Farmland is underwater.

One way to stop floods is to build dams. A dam is a high wall that holds back water. The water a dam holds back makes a lake. In the flood season,

Roosevelt Dam, Arizona

the dam holds back the
extra water. The lake
becomes bigger. Gates in
the dam can be opened
and closed to control the
amount of water in the
river below the dam.

Sometimes when a dam is built, people must move away. Their homes will be covered by the lake.

In Africa, when a dam was built on the Zambezi River, a special problem arose. Thousands of wild animals lived on the land where the lake would be. Men in small boats saved the animals. This life-saving work was called "Operation Noah."

Dams do more than control floods. Some can make electricity. Water behind the dam falls through big pipes. The force of this falling water makes part of a big machine spin around and around. When it spins it makes electricity. Electricity made by waterpower is called hydroelectricity.

Power lines

Power lines carry the electricity to cities and towns that need it.

The big machines are generators. There are many generators in one dam.

HOW WE USE RIVERS

Long ago people who lived along rivers carried water to their homes. The women washed clothes in the river. In some parts of the world people still use rivers this way.

Nile River

Now pipes carry water to most homes and factories.

Before water goes into the pipes, it must be cleaned. Dirt is taken out of it and germs are killed. The river water is made pure enough to drink.

Industrial buildings along the Ohio River

Factories are often built near rivers. Water is used to make many products, such as paint and paper and plastics. Water is also used to cool machines and to carry away waste matter. Too much waste dumped into the rivers has spoiled many of them.

Some cities are far away from the rivers that give them water. Engineers dig ditches, lay big pipes, and cut tunnels to get water to the cities.

Water for cities in southern California comes hundreds of miles over the mountains and deserts. The main source of this water is the Colorado River.

North Fork of the Colorado River

In some parts of the world there is not much rain. There the farmers dig ditches that bring water from the rivers to the fields so crops will grow.

Places that once were dry deserts have been turned into green fields and gardens. One of these places is in Israel. Water from the Jordan River is changing a desert into rich farmland.

RIVERS ARE WATER HIGHWAYS

Before there were roads, rivers were the highways through a country.

Now, people in most parts of the world can travel by train or airplane or car. But many heavy goods, such as coal, steel, grain, sand, and gravel, still

Barge on the Mississippi River

Chemical transport going through a lock on the Welland Canal, part of the St. Lawrence Seaway

go by river. Long strings of barges can be seen going up and down the busy rivers of the world.

Waterfalls and rapids are like roadblocks in a river. Men have built canals and locks so that boats can go around them.

Rivers like the Rhine, the Rhone, and the Seine in Europe are water highways. Canals link the rivers together.

Canals and locks on the
St. Lawrence Seaway make
it possible for ocean ships
to come in to the heart of
North America.

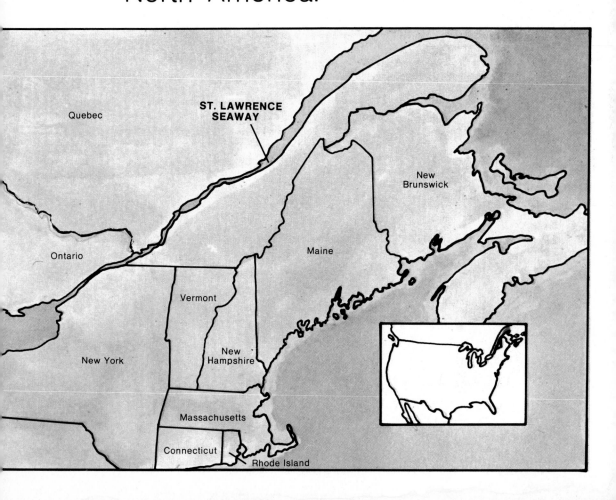

WE NEED CLEAN RIVERS

Once most streams and rivers were clean. They sparkled. Fish swam in them. Small animals lived along the banks.

Now many rivers have been spoiled. People have dumped things into them. The water is dirty. The fish have died.

People must
work together
to keep
rivers clean.

Today people are trying
to make rivers clean again.
Laws have been made
that keep people, factories,
and cities from dumping
waste materials into rivers.

43

You have seen how a river begins, and how it grows and changes the land. You have seen how men use a river's power to make electricity, and how they have used its water to make a desert bloom.

Nile River

Fox River, Illinois

A clean river adds beauty to the land. It can be enjoyed in many ways by everyone.

A river is a wonder of nature. We must work to keep our rivers clean.

WORDS YOU SHOULD KNOW

barge(BARJ)—a flat bottomed boat that carries cargo on rivers and canals

bulk—large quantity; great size

canal(kun • AL)—a body of water, usually created by digging, that connects two or more places

crops—plants grown for food

drain(DRANE)—to have liquid flow off

glacier(GLAY • sher)—a large mass of ice that moves slowly down a valley or mountainside

harness(HAR • ness)—to bring under control

level(LEV • il)—even; flat

lock(LOK)—a part of a river or canal, closed off with gates, in which a ship can be raised or lowered by pumping water in or out

rapids(RAP • idz)—a place in the river where the water flows very quickly

rescue(RESS • kew)—save

roadblock(RODE • blok)—something which blocks movement

spring—a natural flow of water

waste matter—garbage; worthless material

wears(WAIRZ)—removes; cuts away

INDEX

Africa, 29
Amazon River, 8
Andes Mountains, 8
animals, 29,42
Atlantic Ocean, 13
barges, 39
basin, of a river, 11
bends, of a river, 16
California, 36
canals, 39-41
cities, getting water to, 35, 36
cleaning up rivers, 43, 45
cliffs, 23
Colorado River, 21, 36
Continental Divide, 13
crops, 37
dams, 27-31
deltas, 25, 26
deserts, 36, 37, 44
dirty rivers, 35, 42, 43
divides, 12, 13, 14
drinking water, 33
Egypt, 26
electricity, 30, 31, 44
England, 8
Europe, 40
factories, 33, 34, 43
fish, 42
floods, 27
generators, 31

gorges, 18, 19
Grand Canyon, 21
highways, of water, 38-41
hills, 5
hydroelectricity, 30
islands, 16
Israel, 37
Jordan River, 37
lakes, 5, 9, 27, 28
locks, 39, 41
Minnesota, 9
Mississippi River, 9, 10, 26
mountains, 5, 19, 36
New Orleans, 26
Nile River, 26
North America, 41
oceans, 10,13
"Operation Noah," 29
Pacific Ocean, 13
plants, 14
ponds, 5
power lines, 31
products, made using water, 34
rain, 6, 10, 13, 17, 21, 27, 37
rapids, 39
Rhine River, 19, 40
Rhone River, 40
river basins, 11
rocks, 15, 16, 18, 21, 23, 24
Rocky Mountains, 13
St. Lawrence Seaway, 41

sand, 16, 21
seas, 10, 25
Seine River, 40
snow, 6, 17, 27
soil, 15, 17, 25
source, of a river, 5
South America, 8
springs, 5, 8
streams, 6, 8, 10, 14, 19, 42
Thames River, 8
trees, 14

tributaries, 6, 11
United States, 9, 10, 13
uses of rivers, 32-37
valleys, 17
waste, in rivers, 35, 42, 43
waterfalls, 23, 24, 39
water highways, 38-41
water pipes, 33
watersheds, 11, 12, 14
wind, 21
Zambezi River, 29

About the authors

*Freelance authors of magazine articles, Norman and Madelyn
Carlisle have lived in many parts of the United States and
have traveled widely. They have written more than 700
articles for major magazines in the fields of nature,
science, sociology, biography, and history. In their
extensive travels, they had the privilege of being teachers
as well as parents of their six children.*

DATE DUE
